30 AFFIRMATIONS TO ATTRACT FINANCIAL ABUNDANCE

learn how to use your words to create the finance you seek

MIKEL DUKE

COPYRIGHT

©The information contained in this book may not be duplicated, copied, or distributed without the express permission of the author. You are responsible for your own actions, decisions, and outcomes. Several quotes have been rephrased for clarity, and various bible translations have been used for better understanding

About the Author

Mikel Duke is a passionate and motivational writer dedicated to helping others achieve financial freedom and personal growth. With a background in tech and data analytics, Mikel Duke combines practical advice with spiritual wisdom to inspire and empower readers.

Mikel Duke faced numerous financial challenges that shaped his understanding of money and success. Through perseverance, faith, and the power of positive affirmations, He transformed his life from financial drought to abundance. This personal journey inspired Mikel Duke to share his insights with others, leading to the creation of this eBook.

When not writing, Mikel Duke enjoys traveling, reading, acts of philanthropy, spending time with family and friends, and exploring new ways to grow both personally and professionally. Mikel Duke believes in the transformative power of words and is committed to helping readers find hope, strength, and prosperity through their work.

Connect with Mikel Duke on Instagram and X platforms @dukeofafrikaa or send a personal email to mikelduke11@gmail.com for more clarity, resources and inspiration.

TABLE OF CONTENTS

INTRODUCTION
PG.3

AFFIRMATION 1-5
PG.7-11

AFFIRMATION 6-10
PG. 12-16

AFFIRMATION 11-15
PG.17-21

AFFIRMATION 16-20
PG.22-26

AFFIRMATION 21-25
PG. 27-31

AFFIRMATION 26-30
PG.32-36

CONCLUSION
PG.37

INTRODUCTION

Welcome to "30 AFFIRMATIONS TO ATTRACT FINANCIAL ABUNDANCE" An eBook about financial Affirmations and it's importance to our daily lives. This eBook is designed for anyone seeking to improve their financial mindset, break free from financial stagnation, and draw inspiration from the timeless wisdom of the greatest book ever written. Whether you are a young professional, an entrepreneur, or simply someone who desires a healthier relationship with money, this eBook is for you.

I once experienced what felt like an endless financial drought. I struggled to make ends meet and often felt trapped by my circumstances. If this is your current reality, you have found the right book. It was during this challenging period, I discovered a powerful truth: our words have immense power. I realized that my mouth is meant not just for food, but for speaking life into my situation. I discovered that Faith is never silent, and all the written stories of Faith recorded is linked to an "action" that was directly opposite to their situation i.e "Pick up" your mat and walk to a cripple, Calling a man (in his old age) with no child "father of many nations".

The power of affirmations became my lifeline.
I began affirming what I wanted to see in my life despite what I was seeing, using the guiding principles and promises found in the Bible. Over time, I witnessed a remarkable transformation. What started as words of hope and faith began to manifest as tangible changes in my financial situation. It became clear to me that the words we speak are not mere words and they can shape our reality.

This eBook contains 30 daily affirmations, each accompanied by a relevant Bible verse, designed to help you shift your mindset towards financial success, and harness the power of your tongue. By dedicating a few minutes each day to these affirmations, you will start to align your thoughts and actions with the abundance that God promises. Remember, God is not a man that He should lie, therefore everything written in the good book said to be ours, is truly ours, but the second part is you have to agree with it by saying it consistently to see a manifestation.

Let the redeemed of the Lord say so: Yes, You are redeemed but you have to say it.

AFFIRMATION 1

I AM A POWERFUL CREATOR OF ABUNDANCE

BIBLE VERSE

Now to Him who is able to do exceedingly abundantly above all that we ask or think, according to the power that works in us. Ephesians 3:20 (NKJV)

AFFIRMATION 2

I AM A CONDUIT (channel) FOR PROSPERITY.

BIBLE VERSE

Those who live to bless others will have blessings heaped upon them, and the one who pours out his life to pour out blessings will be saturated with favor. Proverbs 11:25 (TPT)

AFFIRMATION 3

I ATTRACT WEALTH AND PROSPERITY WITH EASE

BIBLE VERSE

YOU WILL EAT THE FRUIT OF YOUR LABOR ;BLESSINGS AND PROSPERITY WILL BE YOURS PSALM 128:2(NIV)

AFFIRMATION 4

I AM GRATEFUL FOR THE CONTINOUS FLOW OF MONEY INTO MY LIFE

BIBLE VERSE

Blessed be the Lord,
Who daily loads us with benefits,
The God of our salvation!
Psalm 68:19(NKJV)

AFFIRMATION 5

I AM WISE WITH MY FINANCIAL DECISIONS

BIBLE VERSE

FOR WISDOM WILL ENTER YOUR HEART, AND KNOWLEDGE WILL FILL YOU WITH JOY.
PROVERBS 2:10 (NLT)

AFFIRMATION 6

I AM ATTRACTING OPPORTUNITIES THAT CREATE MORE

BIBLE VERSE

Do you see someone skilled in their work? They will serve before kings; they will not serve before officials of low rank.
Proverbs 22;29(NIV)

AFFIRMATION 7

I FIND SUCCESS IN ALL MY FINANCIAL ENDEAVOURS
BIBLE VERSE

But blessed are those who trust in the Lord
and have made the Lord their hope and confidence.
They are like trees planted along a riverbank,
with roots that reach deep into the water.
**Such trees are not bothered by the heat
or worried by long months of drought.
Their leaves stay green,
and they never stop producing fruit.**
Jeremiah 17 vs 7-8(NLT)

AFFIRMATION 8

My income is constantly increasing

BIBLE VERSE

With me are riches and honor, enduring wealth and prosperity.
PROVERBS 8:18(NIV)

AFFIRMATION 9

I AM CREATING A LIFE OF FINANCIAL FREEDOM AND HAPPINESS

BIBLE VERSE

The blessing of the LORD makes a person rich, and he adds no sorrow with it.

Proverbs 10 vs 22(NLT)

AFFIRMATION 10

PEOPLE LOVE TO HELP ME, I HAVE THE GIFT OF MEN

BIBLE VERSE

Day after day men came to help David, until he had a great army, like the army of God. 1 chronicles 12 vs 22(NIV)

AFFIRMATION 11

I AM FAVOURED BY THE UNIVERSE

BIBLE VERSE
FOR THE LORD GOD IS A SUN AND SHIELD; THE LORD BESTOWS FAVOR AND HONOR; NO GOOD THING DOES HE WITHHOLD FROM THOSE WHOSE WALK IS BLAMELESS. PSALM 84 VS 11(NIV)

Affirmation 12

I AM CAPABLE OF ACHEIVING ANYTHING I SET MY MIND TO DO

BIBLE VERSE

So we may boldly say: "The Lord is my helper; I will not fear. What can man do to me? Hebrews 13:6(NKJV)

AFFIRMATION 13

I am attracting the people linked to my financial next level

BIBLE VERSE

MAY HE GIVE YOU THE DESIRE OF YOUR HEART AND MAKE ALL YOUR PLANS SUCCEED PSALM 20 VS 4(NIV)

AFFIRMATION 14

MY FINANCIAL EXPECTATIONS ARE VALID AND TRANSLATING TO MY CURRENT REALITY

BIBLE VERSE

So do not fear, for I am with you; do not be dismayed, for I am your God. I will strengthen you and help you; I will uphold you with my righteous right hand. Isaiah 41: 10(NLT)

AFFIRMATION 15

I AM WORTHY OF JOYFUL EXPERIENCE THROUGH FINANCIAL ABUNDANCE

BIBLE TEXT
For you make me glad by your deeds, LORD; I sing for joy at what your hands have done. Psalm 92 vs 4(NIV)

AFFIRMATION 16

I AM EMPOWERED TO TURN MY IDEAS INTO PROFITABLE VENTURES

BIBLE VERSE

I am certain that God, who began the good work within you, will continue his work until it is finally finished on the day when Christ Jesus returns.
Philipians 1:6(NLT)

AFFIRMATION 17

I AM FINANCIALLY DISCIPLINED AND RESPONSIBLE

BIBLE TEXT

He holds success in store for the upright, he is a shield to those whose walk is blameless PSALM 2 VS 7(NIV)

AFFIRMATION 18

I AM COMMITED TO GROWING MY FINANCIAL SUCCESS EVERY DAY

BIBLE TEXT
Blessed be the Lord,
Who daily loads us with benefits,
The God of our salvation! Selah. Psalm 68:19 (NKJV)

AFFIRMATION 19

WEALTH AND RICHES ARE IN MY HOUSE

BIBLE VERSE

Wealth and riches are in their houses, and their righteousness endures forever.
PSALM 112 VS 3 (NIV)

AFFIRMATION 20

I AM CONFIDENT IN WHO I AM BECOMING

BIBLE VERSE

This is the confidence we have in approaching God: that if we ask anything according to his will, he hears us.
1JOHN 5 VS 14 (NIV)

AFFIRMATION 21

I AM BLESSED WITH FAVOUR IN ALL AREAS OF MY LIFE

BIBLE VERSE

Surely, Lord, you bless the righteous;
you surround them with your favor as with a shield.
PSALM 5 VS 12 (NKJV)

AFFIRMATION 22

I AM GRATEFUL FOR THE MONEY THAT FLOWS TO ME EASILY AND EFFORTLESSLY

BIBLE VERSE
And this same God who takes care of me will supply all your needs from his glorious riches, which have been given to us in Christ Jesus. Philipians 4:19 (NLT)

AFFIRMATION 23

I AM GRATEFUL FOR OPPORTUNITIES THAT EXPAND MY CAPACITY

BIBLE VERSE
Not that we are competent in ourselves to claim anything for ourselves, but our competence comes from God. 2 CORINTHIANS 3 VS 5(NIV)

AFFIRMATION 24

I AM GRATEFUL FOR THE NEW FINANCIAL DOORS OPENED TO ME

BIBLE VERSE

I know your deeds. See, I have placed before you an open door that no one can shut. I know that you have little strength, yet you have kept my word and have not denied my name.
REVELATION 3 VS 8(NIV)

AFFIRMATION 25

I AM GRATEFUL FOR THE WISDOM TO LEARN FROM BOTH FINANCIAL SUCCESS AND FAILURES

BIBLE VERSE

And we know that in all things God works for the good of those who love him, who have been called according to his purpose
ROMANS 8 VS 28 (NIV).

AFFIRMATION 26

I AM GRATEFUL FOR THE KINDNESS OF STRANGERS

BIBLE VERSE

DO NOT FORGET TO SHOW HOSPITALITY TO STRANGERS, FOR BY SO DOING SOME PEOPLE HAVE SHOWN HOSPITALITY TO ANGELS WITHOUT KNOWING IT. HEBREWS 13:2 (NIV)

AFFIRMATION 27

I AM THANKFUL FOR ROOF OVER MY HEAD AND FOOD ON MY TABLE

BIBLE VERSE
Worship the LORD your God, and his blessing will be on your food and water. I will take away sickness from among you. EXODUS 23 VS 35 (NIV)

AFFIRMATION 28

I AM A SOLUTION TO PROBLEMS

BIBLE VERSE

I CAN DO ALL THINGS THROUGH CHRIST WHO STRENGTHENS ME.

PHILIPIANS 4 VS 13 (NKJV)

AFFIRMATION 29

MY THOUGHTS ARE PURELY FOCUSED ON IMPACTFUL IDEA

BIBLE VERSE

For I know the thoughts that I think toward you, says the Lord, thoughts of peace and not of evil, to give you a future and a hope.
Jeremiah 29 vs 11(NKJV)

AFFIRMATION 30

I AM IN MY GOOD NEWS SEASON

BIBLE VERSE

SURELY YOUR GOODNESS AND LOVE WILL FOLLOW ME ALL THE DAYS OF MY LIFE, AND I WILL DWELL IN THE HOUSE OF THE LORD FOREVER. PSALM 23 VS 6 (NIV)

CONCLUSION

As you begin this journey of daily affirmations, I encourage you to observe and record the changes in your life. Be a student of your life and most importantly, understand that delay is not denial.

The first thing you may notice once you start affirming is that things might initially seem to get worse. Yes, This is a common experience and often a strategy by the enemy to discourage you from continuing your affirmations. Think about it: if affirmations doesn't work, why would there be such resistance immediately you started speaking? Why doesn't the enemy want you to persist?

Stay assured and steadfast. Consistently stick to your affirmations and KNOW that "delay is not denial". Remember, no thief attacks an empty house so the enemy's resistance is a sign that you are on the right path, one that leads to financial breakthrough and abundance.

I want you to keep speaking these affirmations with faith and conviction. Over time, it is inevitable that you will see the fruits of your declarations. Remember, the power of life and death is in the tongue, and your words have the power to shape your reality.

Believe in the process, stay committed, and watch as your financial landscape transforms. Your journey to financial freedom and abundance starts with the words you speak TODAY. Start affirming, stay encouraged, and witness the power of faith-filled words in your life.

www.ingramcontent.com/pod-product-compliance
Lightning Source LLC
Chambersburg PA
CBHW072055230526
45479CB00010B/1085